JO

God

Told by Carine Mackenzie
Illustrations by Fred Apps

Published by Christian Focus Publications
Geanies House, Tain, Ross-shire, IV20 1TW, Scotland
Copyright © 1998 Carine Mackenzie. Reprinted 2004
Printed in China

Joseph was the favourite son of his father Jacob. He had ten older brothers, one sister and one younger brother Benjamin. Benjamin was special because their mother Rachel had died when he was born.

Jacob gave Joseph a beautiful coloured coat to show how much he loved him.

The older brothers were jealous when they saw this. They hated Joseph. They only spoke to him with angry words.

One day Joseph told his brothers about a dream
he had had. 'We were all tying up the corn into
bundles in the field,' he said. 'My bundle stood
up straight and tall but yours all bowed
down in front of mine.'

His brothers were even more angry.
'Do you think that means we will bow
down to you one day?' they demanded.
Joseph had another dream. He told his brothers
and his father about it. 'In my dream the sun,
the moon and eleven stars all bowed to me.'
Did this mean that he would be more
important than all his family?
His brothers envied him even more.

As the brothers were looking after the sheep in a place far from home, Jacob decided to send Joseph to see how they were getting on. Joseph had to travel quite far to find them. The brothers noticed him coming in the distance. They hatched a wicked plot.

'Let's kill Joseph and throw his body in a pit. What will his dreams mean then?' they said.

But one brother called Reuben said, 'Don't kill him. Just throw him in the pit.'

So Joseph's beautiful coat was torn off him and he was flung into a horrible deep dark hole.

Reuben's plan was to rescue Joseph later and let him go back to his father but while Reuben was busy elsewhere, a group of travelling merchants came along with their camels laden with goods. They were on their way to Egypt.

Brother Judah had an idea. 'Let's sell Joseph as a slave to these merchants. We will make some money. Besides it would not be good to kill our own brother.'

Joseph was pulled out of the pit – not to freedom – but to be sold for 20 pieces of silver to the merchants.

Soon he was on his way as a slave to far away Egypt.

The brothers told lies to Joseph's father when they went home. He believed that a wild animal had eaten Joseph. He was heartbroken.

But Joseph was still alive. He was sold as a slave to Potiphar, an important captain of the guard in Pharaoh, the king's, army.

God was with Joseph in this difficult situation. He worked well for his master and Potiphar saw this and rewarded him for his good work.

Potiphar's wife made up a false story about Joseph, accusing him of a wicked deed which he had not done at all. But Potiphar believed his wife and had Joseph thrown into prison.

God was with Joseph in prison too. He was soon given a position of trust by the prison guards.

Pharaoh's butler and baker were in prison under Joseph's charge. One night they both had a vivid dream which troubled them. They did not know what they meant.

'God will help me to give you the meaning,' said Joseph.

Joseph told the butler that within three days he would have his old job back in Pharaoh's palace. The baker's dream did not have such a happy meaning but both did come true.

'Please tell Pharaoh about me,' Joseph said to the butler as he went back to the palace. 'He might get me out of this prison.'

But the butler forgot all about Joseph.

Two years passed and still Joseph was in prison. But God was with Joseph.

One night Pharaoh had two dreams. He did not know what they meant. His wise men could not tell him either. Pharaoh was bothered.

All of a sudden the butler remembered Joseph in the prison. 'I know a man in the prison who was able to tell the meaning of my dream,' he told Pharaoh.

Pharaoh sent immediately for Joseph. Joseph shaved and dressed and went to see Pharaoh.

'God will give you an answer,' he said. And that is what happened. Joseph explained the dream

God was telling Pharaoh - 'There will be seven years of plenty in the land, but then seven years of severe famine.'

Joseph gave Pharaoh good advice.

'Find a wise man to organise the crops that are grown during the seven years of plenty. He should save part of the crop to be used later when food is scarce.'

Pharaoh thought that was a great idea. Where could he find such a good wise man?

Why, Joseph, of course. He would be just the right man.

So Pharaoh gave Joseph this important job. He gave him a ring for his finger, beautiful clothes and a gold chain round his neck. He was given a chariot to ride in. He was now a ruler in the land of Egypt – a very important man.

Life was very different for Joseph now. He married Asenath and they had two little boys, Ephraim and Manasseh. Joseph did his job well and gathered lots of grain in the big storehouses.

When the famine came, the people needed food. They went to Pharaoh for help and he said, 'Go to Joseph.' People came from all over to get bread. They came even from the land of Canaan, Joseph's old home country.

One day, ten of Joseph's brothers arrived to buy bread. They fell down before the important ruler of Egypt to ask for food, not realising that he was their brother Joseph.

The dream had come true.

Joseph recognised his brothers but he did not tell them who he was. He spoke roughly to them. 'You are spies.'

'Oh no!' they replied. 'We have just come to buy food. We are all brothers. Our youngest brother is with our father back home.'

'One of you go and fetch him here then,' said Joseph, 'and I'll keep the rest of you in prison.'

So he put them in prison for three days.

Then he relented and allowed them to go back for Benjamin on condition that one brother stayed in prison.

Joseph overheard his brothers speaking among themselves. 'We are being punished for our treatment of our brother Joseph,' they confessed. They did not realise that Joseph could understand them perfectly, because up till then he had spoken through an interpreter.

So Simeon remained in Egypt while the rest went off with plenty of corn in their sacks.

To their surprise their money was found at the top of their sacks too. The brothers reported everything to their father when they got home. He was amazed at the story but refused to let Benjamin go. Eventually the food ran short. The family was starving.

Someone would have to go back to Egypt for more supplies.

'Benjamin will have to come if we are to get any food. We will look after him,' they promised.

So their father reluctantly agreed. 'Take the man some presents. Make sure you have double money to make up for last time,' was their father's advice.

The brothers returned to Egypt and this time Benjamin was with them.

Joseph was delighted to see his young brother. He invited them all to his own home for a feast. Simeon was brought out of the prison. All the brothers again bowed down before Joseph. He sat them down at the table in order of their ages. They all had a wonderful meal but Benjamin's share was five times larger than anyone else's.

Still Joseph did not tell them who he was. He had to test them further.

Joseph gave the order to his servant – 'Fill the men's sacks with corn, put their money back in the sacks again and put my silver cup in the sack belonging to the youngest man.'

So the brothers set off for home. Soon some of Joseph's men came chasing after them, accusing them of stealing Joseph's silver cup. 'We would never do that. You can kill whoever has a silver cup in his sack. Search us all,' they claimed confidently. What a shock they got when the cup was found in Benjamin's sack.

They returned to Joseph in a terrible state. What would happen now?

Judah stepped up to Joseph to plead for young Benjamin. 'Punish me instead. Please let him go back to his father. It would kill his father if anything happened to him.'

Joseph could not hide it any longer. He had to tell them who he was. He sent all the servants out of the room.

'I am Joseph,' he said. 'Is my father still alive?'

The brothers could not answer a word. They were so surprised and troubled.

'Please come near me,' Joseph said. 'I am Joseph your brother, whom you sold to Egypt. Do not be unhappy or angry with yourselves that you did that, because God sent me here to save many lives and to save your lives.

Go back to fetch our father. You can all live here in this country. I will look after you all.'

He kissed them all weeping. Then his brothers were able to talk to him.

Joseph sent his brothers back to fetch his father and all their family. He gave them big carts to carry everyone, and lots of food and new clothes and presents. 'See that you do not start to quarrel on the way home,' he warned them.

What news they had for Jacob their old father when they got home.

'Joseph is still alive. He is ruler of all the land of Egypt.'

Jacob could not believe it. They told him all that Joseph had said and then when he saw the big carts sent to fetch him, he finally believed them.

'I will go and see my son Joseph again before I die,' he said.

Jacob made the long journey to Egypt. Joseph went to meet his father again after so many years. They hugged each other and wept for a long time.

Joseph's family was given the best of the land to settle in and they prospered there.

After their father had died, Joseph's brothers were afraid that he would turn against them. But he spoke kindly to them. 'Do not be afraid. You intended to harm me, but God intended it for good – to save many lives.'

God's purpose in sending Joseph to Egypt was to save many people including his family. God's purpose in sending Jesus to this world was to save the people who believe in him from their sins and give them eternal life.